DUCK EGGS

Copyright © 2015 by Emily Lane Waszak

Measure of Success Productions

Canton, MI 48187

For Great Ga—As promised, I am sharing the story. And for Robert, Luke, Cassidy, Ainsley, and Levi...may your lives be filled with many stories to share with others. - ELW

To my husband, David, for all of the love, support, and care. - OB

While visiting at Grandma's house, Cassidy climbed up to the table to watch her make the biscuits. As Grandma put them into the oven, Cassidy asked, "How much time do we have before dinner, Grandma?" "Oh, about twenty minutes," she answered. "Do you think we have time for an interview, Grandma?" Cassidy wanted to use the tape recorder she had received as a Christmas gift.

"An interview? Well, I suppose. I don't know why you would want to interview me, though," she said with a curious chuckle. Grandma and Cassidy walked into Grandma's bedroom and sat on the bed. "We'll be more comfortable in here, I'm sure," Grandma said. Cassidy set up the tape recorder and pressed the big red button. The tape began to slowly turn, and Cassidy held the microphone up to her mouth. "Grandma, what is one of your favorite memories as a child?" Grandma took the microphone and began to speak.

"There was something I used to do with my Daddy. One day, he was hot and tired. He had been working up in the field, and when he came down, he said, 'Let's you and I go fishing.' Of course, I could never refuse fishing with my Daddy. We cut our fishing poles as we walked along. You see, we didn't have those fancy poles like you have today. We had to fetch a good long branch and make our pole on the way."

"We went down to what we called 'the branch' - it was a little creek. As we cut through Mr. Beardsley's place, I saw something lying in the tall grass. It didn't look like a baseball that I would sometimes find in the field, and I couldn't imagine what it could be. It was a little larger than a chicken egg, and it was kind of blue looking. I said, 'Oh Poppa, what is this that I have found?'"

"He said, 'Why, that's a duck egg.' And I said, 'Well, there's another, and another, and ANOTHER!'" Grandma's excitement grew with each word. "There were about a dozen duck eggs. I had a little apron on over my skirt, and I gathered it and placed the first egg in there. As I walked along, I picked up another one and another one, and I asked, 'Poppa, is it wrong to take them? Is it stealing?'"

"And he said, 'Oh no, no, because if you don't pick these up, we don't know what will happen to them. They will probably just lie here in the hot sun and rot.'"

"Some duck has come along here and laid eggs, and we don't know whose duck it was. So that's all right for you to take them. Now you go ahead and feel free.'"

"So I did. I gathered them all, and then I gently laid my little duck eggs down and fished with my Daddy. When we had finished, I carefully picked them back up when it was time to go, and I carried them home."

"As we came closer to the house, I yelled, 'Oh, Momma! Guess what we've got!' She came to the door and said, 'Why, Hilda, those are duck eggs! Where did you get them?' I told her the story, and she said, 'Well, I have a chicken setting, and I'll set your duck eggs under the hen, and she'll hatch them.'"

"Well, I watched, and after three weeks had passed, she always hatched her own chickens. The ducks hadn't even started pipping. I know that old hen thought that she was not going to have any chickens at all. But she sat there another week until they finally hatched. They were little bitty ducks with little bitty yellow duck bills. They were the cutest little things you ever did see."

"She wondered why her chickens didn't follow her when she would motion to them. They didn't act like her other chickens. And when they wandered down to the branch, the little ducks jumped into the water and swam."

"She had to stand there and watch them, and I bet she thought, 'Boy, is my face red. I don't know what I have here, but I haven't chickens, that's for sure! They can swim and I can't.'"

"My Daddy told me, 'Now those are your ducks, and you have to watch them.' Well, they would run away to the neighbor's pasture. I would have to chase them and drive them home with a stick, but when they got to the water, they would want to swim. They grew to be good-sized ducks, and my Daddy thought that he had better take them to market. He told me, 'I'll give you the money.' He took the ducks, put them in a coop, took them to Bedford, and people bought them."

"And do you know what? I made enough money from those ducks that I was able to buy myself a new winter coat. It was this beautiful purple coat that I had wanted for a long time.

At that moment, the timer on the oven sounded, and Cassidy turned the tape recorder off. "Thank you, Grandma," she said. "You're welcome," Grandma replied, with a smile on her face and a gleam in her eye. The memory had made Grandma so happy. "You just be sure to share that story with your children and your grandchildren someday, Cassidy."

"I will, Grandma. I will."

Emily Lane Waszak began writing as a child, and she continues to share this passion as a college instructor. When she is not writing or teaching, she is volunteering in the local schools. Her first book, "Grief: Difficult Times, Simple Steps"(Taylor & Francis), was inspired by her volunteer work at a grief center for children. She is currently active in writing instructional texts for educators, including her latest releases with Erik Bean, "Word Press for Student Writing Projects" (Brigantine Media, Compass Publishing Division, St. Johnsbury, VT) and "Social Media Writing Lesson Plans" (Westphalia Press, Washington, D.C.) as well as several upcoming children's books. She resides in Michigan with her husband, Jeremy, and their five children.

Olga Baruk has enjoyed drawing as long as she can remember, since her childhood in Russia. She likes to leave a magical touch and special details in her drawings to remind little readers and their parents alike that anyone is able to create his or her own sense of mystic in everyday life. She is married with three children who all share her passion and artistic talent. Olga is a registered nurse, and she enjoys sharing her art with her patients. She often creates custom drawings for them for comfort and peace. She looks forward to amusing you with future art projects.

Watch for upcoming titles by Emily Lane Waszak:

"Chief Little Red Cheeks" - **Get ready for an adventure with "Chief Little Red Cheeks", a little boy full of spunk and wonder. Both children and adults alike will delight in this tale of exploration of the world around them. Sit back and enjoy a quest into the woods of Northern Michigan, because after all, you never know what you are going to run into out there!**

"Whitetail Picnic" - **An endearing tale following a young boy and his mother as they share an appreciation of nature's beauty and a special time together.**

www.ingramcontent.com/pod-product-compliance
Lightning Source LLC
Chambersburg PA
CBHW041346290326
41933CB00036B/178

* 9 7 8 0 6 9 2 5 5 2 2 5 4 *